DISCARD

4x4 Trucks

BY DENNY VON FINN

BELLWETHER MEDIA • MINNEAPOLIS, MN

Are you ready to take it to the extreme?

Torque books thrust you into the action-packed world of sports, vehicles, and adventure. These books may include dirt, smoke, fire, and dangerous stunts.

WARNING: READ AT YOUR OWN RISK.

This edition first published in 2009 by Bellwether Media, Inc.

No part of this publication may be reproduced in whole or in part without written permission of the publisher. For information regarding permission, write to Bellwether Media, Inc., Attention: Permissions Department, 5357 Penn Avenue South, Minneapolis, MN 55419.

Library of Congress Cataloging-in-Publication Data
Von Finn, Denny.
 4 x 4 trucks / by Denny Von Finn.
   p. cm. — (Torque. Cool rides)
 Includes bibliographical references and index.
 Summary: "Full-color photography accompanies engaging information about 4x4 trucks. The combination of high-interest subject matter and light text is intended for students in grades 3 through 7"—Provided by publisher.
  ISBN: 978-1-60014-254-3 (hardcover : alk. paper)
 1. Four-wheel drive trucks—Juvenile literature. I. Title.

TL230.5.F6V66 2009
629.223—dc22   2008035640

Printed in the United States of America, North Mankato, MN

Contents

What Is a 4x4 Truck?

A **4x4** truck is a vehicle designed to handle rough terrain, climb steep hills, and tow heavy loads. Some 4x4 trucks even crawl over large rocks. These tough vehicles are sometimes just called "four by fours."

The term "4x4" means that a truck's four wheels receive equal amounts of power. The truck has **driveshafts** that power all four wheels at the same time. This is called **four-wheel drive**. Four-wheel drive gives a vehicle better **traction**.

Fast Fact

Four-wheel drive makes a vehicle more stable. For this reason, forms of four-wheel drive have long been used in sports cars and race cars.

Most trucks have just one driveshaft. This sends power to only the rear wheels. A 4x4 truck has two driveshafts. The rear driveshaft sends power to the rear wheels. The front driveshaft sends power to the front wheels. A 4x4 driver can turn on four-wheel drive using a lever or a switch.

4x4 Truck History

The first 4x4s were built more than 100 years ago. During World War I, 4x4 trucks helped soldiers move heavy loads. Four-wheel drive trucks were also useful in the **off-road** conditions near battlegrounds.

A company called Willys-Overland Motors began building the **Jeep** for the United States Army in 1941. This small 4x4 was very popular with American soldiers. The first Jeep for everyday use was made in 1945.

Fast Fact

More than 600,000 Jeeps were produced from 1941 to 1945 for use in World War II.

Parts Of a 4x4 Truck

Four-wheel drive is only one feature that helps a 4x4 tackle tough terrain. A 4x4 truck's **suspension system** includes springs and shock absorbers. On rough terrain, the suspension system moves to make the ride less bumpy.

Fast FaCt

Fast FaCt

Monster trucks are 4x4 trucks with enormous tires. The monster truck Bigfoot is perhaps the most famous 4x4 truck ever.

Many 4x4 truck owners also install a **lift kit**. This raises the truck's body and provides more **ground clearance**. This additional distance between the ground and the body also allows for larger tires.

A 4x4 truck driver can use different tires for different terrain. Some tires are designed for sand. Other tires are made for snow. There are also tires that help trucks climb rocks and drive through mud.

Drivers often let some air out of their tires. This makes them softer. Hard tires can bounce on several kinds of terrain. Bouncing tires make a 4x4 difficult to steer.

A 4x4 owner has many **aftermarket** parts to choose from. Some of these parts, such as a new body, give a 4x4 truck a unique look. Other aftermarket parts are very useful. A **winch**, for example, is a handy device when a 4x4 truck gets stuck.

4x4 Trucks in Action

Most 4x4 owners use their vehicles to have fun. Some owners participate in **rock crawling**. This sport features short courses filled with boulders and rock piles. The speeds are slow, but the courses require great skill to navigate successfully.

Fast FaCt

The Rubicon Trail is a legendary off-road route in northern California. It is 22 miles (35 kilometers) long and a popular destination for 4x4 enthusiasts.

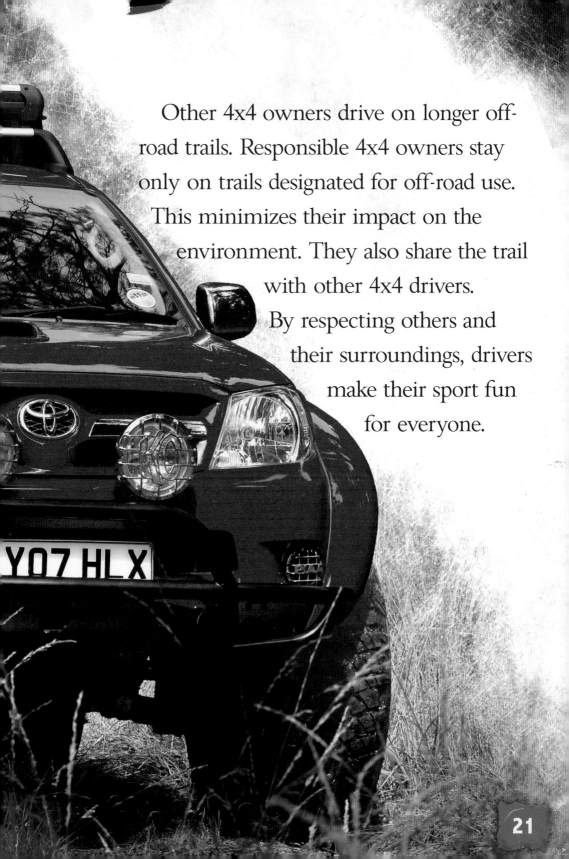

Other 4x4 owners drive on longer off-road trails. Responsible 4x4 owners stay only on trails designated for off-road use. This minimizes their impact on the environment. They also share the trail with other 4x4 drivers. By respecting others and their surroundings, drivers make their sport fun for everyone.

Glossary

4x4—a vehicle with four wheels that are all capable of receiving power

aftermarket—refers to specialized parts that are added to a vehicle after it leaves the factory where it was built

driveshafts—mechanisms that transfer power from the engine to the wheels

four-wheel drive—a feature that allows all four of a truck's wheels to receive power from the engine

ground clearance—the distance between the ground and the bottom of a vehicle's body

Jeep—a popular brand of 4x4 first built for the United States Army in World War II

lift kit—a system of springs and shocks that raises a vehicle's body

off-road—a driving surface that is not paved

rock crawling—a sport in which drivers navigate short courses filled with boulders, rock piles, and other obstacles

suspension system—the springs and shock absorbers that connect the body of a 4x4 to its wheels

traction—the grip between the tires of a vehicle and the ground; traction helps the vehicle move forward.

winch—a spool-like device that uses a cable to pull or lift

To Learn More

AT THE LIBRARY

Morganelli, Adrianna. *Trucks: Pickups to Big Rigs*. New York: Crabtree, 2007.

Zobel, Derek. *Monster Vehicles*. Minneapolis, Minn.: Bellwether, 2008.

Zuehlke, Jeffrey. *Pickup Trucks*. Minneapolis, Minn.: Lerner, 2007.

ON THE WEB

Learning more about 4x4 trucks is as easy as 1, 2, 3.

1. Go to www.factsurfer.com.

2. Enter "4x4 trucks" into the search box.

3. Click the "Surf" button and you will see a list of related Web sites.

With factsurfer.com, finding more information is just a click away.

Index

The images in this book are reproduced through the courtesy of: Juan Martinez, front cover; Byllwill, pp. 4-5, 16-17 (lower); © PhotoStockFile / Alamy, pp. 6-7; Michaela Stejskalova, pp. 8-9; © Jazavac, p. 10; © imagebroker / Alamy, p. 11; Devin Koob, p. 12; Michael Stokes, p. 13; © PhotoStockFile / Alamy, p. 14; Jacom Stephens, p. 15; Raymond Gregory, p. 17 (upper); Jason Lugo, pp. 18-19; © Motoring Picture Library / Alamy, pp. 20-21.

Jefferson Lincoln Elementary

400 W. Summa

Centralia, Washington

360 - 330 -7636

128693 EN
4x4 Trucks

Von Finn, Denny
ATOS BL 3.9
Points: 0.5